E
Is for
Ethics

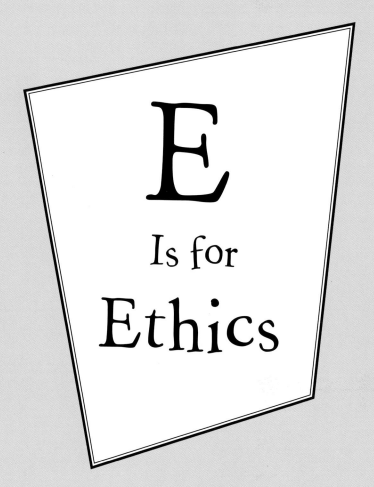

E

Is for

Ethics

How to Talk to Kids About Morals, Values, and What Matters Most

ℰℓℊ

Ian James Corlett

Illustrated by R. A. Holt

ATRIA BOOKS

New York   London   Toronto   Sydney

ATRIA BOOKS

A Division of Simon & Schuster, Inc.

1230 Avenue of the Americas

New York, NY 10020

Copyright © 2009 by Ian James Corlett

First Atria Books hardcover edition December 2009

ATRIA BOOKS and colophon are trademarks of Simon & Schuster, Inc.

For information about special discounts for bulk purchases, please contact Simon & Schuster Special Sales at 1-866-506-1949 or business@simonandschuster.com.

The Simon & Schuster Speakers Bureau can bring authors to your live event. For more information or to book an event contact the Simon & Schuster Speakers Bureau at 1-866-248-3049 or visit our website at www.simonspeakers.com.

Designed by Nancy Singer

Manufactured in China

10 9 8 7 6 5 4 3 2 1

Library of Congress Cataloging-in-Publication Data

ISBN 978-1-4165-9654-7
ISBN 978-1-4165-9669-1 (ebook)

For Philip and Claire—
Love, Dad

Contents

Foreword

To write a book on ethics, or "the science of morals" as they have been called, is a pretty lofty aspiration. Surely, the writer should be serious and lettered. Definitely, he should be qualified. I most certainly am qualified: I am proud to be a POD. Now, I know what you're thinking: *He meant PHD.* Nope. No mistake. I'm a POD.

POD stands for Plain Old Dad.

Yes, I'm just a dad. I'm a plain old dad with no degree, no letters, nothin'. I'm like the guy in the old XTC song "Mayor of Simpleton" who "never took a paper or a learned degree."

So, now you know what I *don't* have. What I *do* have are two amazing children, running around my house begging for guidance and direction.

As a plain old dad, along with their mother, it was my responsibility to provide that to our kids.

My wife and I firmly agree with experts who contend that much of a child's personality and characteristics are formed at a very young age.

Ever since our children were very small, our family has sat down every week for a discussion period we affectionately call "family fun time." We discuss ideas, parables, and issues of the week. For a few minutes every Monday night, this has been our routine.

As we shared this routine with other parents, their eyes lit up, and they said things like "What a great idea!" and "Wow, that's perfect" and "Doesn't that cut into *Monday Night Football*?"

So, I decided to write this book.

Historically, ethics were imparted to children by authority figures. There was a time when ethics were routinely taught in schools, but for the most part, ethics are not part of any curriculum today, even religious ones. It seems that no one wants to touch the subject of right and wrong anymore. I believe that parents should and must fill this void, and I think most parents would agree, regardless of creed, political stripe, or culture.

In this book, you will find twenty-six stories, each of which demonstrates a different ethic or value. Once a week, sit down with your kids and read and talk about one. Set a day, set a time, and stick to it. It doesn't have to be formal, and remember to keep things light and fun. If you stick to your schedule, you'll cover it twice in a year (I was a C+ math student).

After each story, there is a short commentary and quotes from famous individuals. This wrap-up is designed to help parents open up discussion on the subject.

I firmly believe that children need training, reinforcement, and respect for ethics. I think this book is a baby step in the right direction. I hope you agree.

Ian

E

Is for

Ethics

1

Honesty

It was a rainy winter day. Elliott was walking to the video store with his mother to pick up a movie for the evening. Mom was looking for a light comedy to watch with Dad as the fireplace crackled, but Elliott had nothing but spaceships on his mind. That is, until he noticed a crisp, new five-dollar bill lying on the ground at the entrance to the shop. His mother didn't see it as she entered the video store, but Elliott locked on it like a tractor beam. Since no one was around, he picked it up and shoved it deep into his pocket.

As he drifted toward the "Outer Space" section, Elliott could not believe his good luck. He could hardly concentrate on selecting a movie because he was daydreaming about all the wild and wonderful ways he could spend his newfound fortune. He wandered around in such a daze that he didn't even realize that not only had he not chosen a movie, but he was now standing in the checkout line beside his mother, who was waiting to pay.

Suddenly, his daydream was shattered when the lady in front of them, who was frantically searching through her purse, gasped. "I am positive I had five dollars," she said. "I know because I just got a nice, crisp one in change from the last store . . . Oh, heavens! It must've dropped out of my bag!"

Elliott's heart sank. Would he be *honest* and give the lady the five-dollar bill?

QUESTION

What would be the HONEST thing for Elliott to do?

As with so many ethical qualities, being honest makes you feel great inside. Sometimes it's difficult to be honest with others or even yourself, but when you are, there is no better way of life. Elliott felt great when he was guided by *honesty* about the money.

MORE QUESTIONS

- What else could Elliott have done as soon as he found the five-dollar bill?
- How would Elliott have felt later if he had decided to keep the five dollars?
- Can you tell us about a situation you can remember when you or a friend displayed honesty?

"Honesty is the best policy."
WILLIAM SHAKESPEARE

"Honesty: The best of all the lost arts."
MARK TWAIN

2

Understanding

Lucy adored her aunt Shannon. She was the fun aunt. On each visit, there would be ice cream, bookstores, bike rides, and sometimes all of them at once!

Aunt Shannon was coming on the weekend to pick Lucy up for a "girls-only" sleepover. "This is going to be the best, most superfantastic weekend of my life!" exclaimed Lucy. She was so excited as she ran up to her room and stuffed her bright pink suitcase with her favorite dresses, toys, and treats. Lucy was packed and ready to go days ahead of time. She could hardly sleep waiting for the weekend to come.

Saturday morning finally arrived. Lucy was up early, dressed for the chilly weather and waiting at the door. In the background, Lucy could hear her mother on the phone. When she hung up, she moved quietly toward Lucy. Lucy sensed that something was wrong and instinctively scowled and braced herself. "Lucy, I have some bad news. Your aunt Shannon has to cancel your weekend."

Lucy's eyes welled up with tears. She felt as if time had stopped and her world was coming to an end. Her mom explained that Aunt Shannon's best friend had sprained her ankle on a jog and needed to go to the hospital for X-rays. Aunt Shannon had to take her there, and she hoped that Lucy would *understand*. She also wanted Lucy to know that she promised to have her over the next weekend. This was all very difficult for Lucy, who was feeling very sad.

QUESTION

How could Lucy show that she is UNDERSTANDING?

Sometimes it's difficult to understand other people's actions. But the best thing to do is ask yourself, "How would I feel if I were in their place?" Poor Lucy must have found it hard to *understand* that her aunt felt a responsibility to help her friend, especially when it meant ruining her weekend. Rest assured, she had a great time when they finally did have their "girls-only" sleepover together!

MORE QUESTIONS

- ◉ How do you think Aunt Shannon felt about canceling?
- ◉ Have you ever felt disappointed about something?
- ◉ Has someone ever been understanding to you?
- ◉ Have there been situations where you have needed to be understanding?

"Understanding is a two-way street."
ELEANOR ROOSEVELT

*"The noblest pleasure is the joy
of understanding."*
LEONARDO DA VINCI

*"No law or ordinance is mightier
than understanding."*
PLATO

3

∽∾

Forgiveness

Elliott and Lucy were both playing in the living room with their Danish-made generic building blocks. Lucy was busy building an elaborate toy doggie spa, complete with walk-in shower stalls, bunk beds, and a tall sign that would bring in customers from miles around. (Well, as far away as the kitchen, perhaps.) Meanwhile, Elliott was busy designing the most awesome star fighter the galaxy has ever seen. He zoomed it around the room with gusto and sound effects. As he dipped and dove, he got closer and closer to Lucy's towering sign, until—*clllack!* He clipped it.

Elliott froze. The sign teetered to the left. He looked at Lucy. The sign teetered to the right. Lucy looked on in shock and horror. Elliott braced for the worst. Finally, the tower teetered too far and toppled into a hundred pieces, scattering across the living-room floor.

"I'm so sorry, Lucy!" blurted Elliott.

Lucy looked angry and shouted, "You did this on purpose! You ruined my doggie spa!" Her anger soon turned to sadness as her eyes welled up with tears.

Elliott realized how truly hurt she was and moved to put his arm around her. "I was just careless, Lucy. I was too busy having fun to notice." Lucy sniffed back a tear. "I didn't mean to wreck your tower, but I can help you rebuild it. I'm sorry. Please forgive me?"

Lucy realized that Elliott was sincere in his apology, but she was still very upset.

QUESTION

How could Lucy show FORGIVENESS?

Forgiveness is a challenge for most of us. We may have heard the expression "Forgive and forget," which really means to move on. It would be unreasonable to expect our memory to be wiped clean of something nasty that someone did to us, but if we really forgive from inside our heart, we won't bring it up again.

MORE QUESTIONS

◉ What would have happened if Lucy hadn't forgiven Elliott?
◉ Is it easier to forgive a friend rather than a brother or sister? Or to forgive a child rather than a grown-up?
◉ Is there anything you still hold a grudge about?
◉ When did you last forgive somebody?

"The weak can never forgive.
Forgiveness is the attribute of the strong."
MAHATMA GANDHI

"Always forgive your enemies;
nothing annoys them so much."
OSCAR WILDE

4

Courage

Lana was a new girl at school. Being in new surroundings, she kept to herself. It's always tough to make friends at a new school, and it's even tougher when someone looks as unfriendly as Lana. Yes, poor Lana was one of those people who just looked as if she crunched up gravel for breakfast and swallowed it down with lemon juice. To make matters worse, she had a single thick, dark eyebrow on her forehead, which made her look as if she actually enjoyed scaring people!

Consequently, everyone in the school completely avoided her. In fact, she was so scary-looking that before the end of her very first day, some of the kids were telling frightening stories about her. Clarissa said she came from a family of professional wrestlers and that if you tried to shake hands with her, she'd flip you over her shoulder and put you straight into a toehold! Bianca said she'd heard that Lana was so mean that if you even said hello, she would reply by shooting flames out of her eyes and scorch you! Tall tales, for sure, but as untrue as they were, no one in the school was welcoming her.

Elliott heard the stories too but decided that they had to be made up. Really, who has *both* parents who are wrestlers? Elliott remembered a story his dad once told him about an old lady named Phyllis. He said that Phyllis was the grumpiest-looking person on the outside, but on the inside, she was a sweet and kind lady. He remembered something else his father had told him. "Always show courage, Elliott," he had said, "and never be afraid to take on something difficult." Elliott reasoned that this all sounded a lot like the Lana situation. He had another look at uni-browed Lana, took a deep breath, and then . . .

QUESTION

What do you think Elliott did next that showed COURAGE?

Sometimes things are not as they appear. Sometimes they seem even scary. But even though it takes courage to confront something or someone, it is usually worth the effort. Elliott found out that Lana was actually a really nice, friendly, funny girl, who ended up being a good friend. Soon, because of Elliott's courage, everyone in the school learned that the scary-looking girl could not be any nicer!

MORE QUESTIONS

- Have you ever had to show courage?
- Have you ever had to meet someone you thought was scary?
- Talk about some acts of courage that you have seen or heard about.
- Do you know of someone who always tries to show courage?

> *"Courage is going from failure to failure without losing enthusiasm."*
> WINSTON CHURCHILL
>
> *"Courage is resistance to fear, mastery of fear—not absence of fear."*
> MARK TWAIN

5

∞

Tact

Every February, Elliott's dad took him to visit the dentist. Elliott was concerned. Elliott was worried. Elliott was just a little scared too. But Elliott didn't fear the dentist or his drill. He feared his breath.

Elliott said that Dr. Mowlar had the stinkiest breath on the earth. It was always as if he'd had garlic, sardines, and a dead cat for lunch. Elliott confessed this to his dad, who asked Elliott what he was going to do. Elliott's solution was not to go to the dentist. That was not an option, so Dad set up a role-playing situation. Elliott would play Dr. Mowlar, and Dad would be Elliott.

Dr. Mowlar (Elliott) leaned over Elliott (Dad) and exhaled. Dad cringed.

Elliott asked, "What's the matter, young man, are you afraid of the dentist?"

Dad replied, "Yeah, I'm afraid of your stinky garbage-dump breath!" Elliott laughed.

Then Dad tried another one. "Um, yes, I'm cringing because I'm really afraid of the dentist!"

Elliott knew that was a lie.

Then Dad asked Elliott to be the dentist one more time. Elliott leaned in and breathed on Dad again, and when Dad cringed and Elliott asked what the problem was, Dad simply reached into his pocket, pulled out a nice, fresh breath mint, and held it out to Elliott (Dr. Mowlar). Dad simply smiled and didn't say a word.

Elliott didn't know what to say, so Dad jumped in. "Dr. Mowlar will most likely say, 'Why, thank you, Elliott! Everyone needs a breath mint now and then!'"

Both Elliott and his dad shared a big laugh, and Elliott now knew exactly what to do!

QUESTION

Which of Dad's ideas was the one showing TACT?

Elliott was legitimately repulsed by his dentist's breath, but was it just an excuse to get out of going to the dentist? Dad's first idea was really funny but would surely hurt the dentist's feelings. The second one was pretty much a lie. The third one solved the situation without Elliott even needing to say a word. That is *tact* in action.

MORE QUESTIONS

◉ Think of a situation when you have shown tact.
◉ How do you think Elliott would feel if he lied to the dentist?
◉ Has someone ever treated you with tact?
◉ How many different ways can you think of to get rid of bad breath?

> *"Tact is the art of making a point without making an enemy."*
> SIR ISAAC NEWTON
>
> *"Tact is the ability to describe others as they see themselves."*
> ABRAHAM LINCOLN

6

Perseverance

Lucy enjoyed playing the piano. She loved the feeling of using her tiny fingers to make a big musical sound. She liked entertaining guests with the latest song she had mastered. Today, Lucy was learning to play "Rainy Day," a difficult song but appropriate, since it had been raining solid for what seemed like a month. Lucy struggled as her mom helped her through the first time. Lucy especially had difficulty reaching the F-sharp with her little pinky, yelling, "It's impossible!"

Every time she practiced the song, she got a little bit better. Her mom kept encouraging her to keep trying, but no matter how much she improved, when she got to the F-sharp near the end, she just couldn't reach it.

Lucy got more and more frustrated and proclaimed to her mom, "I'm quitting!"

Her mom knew that Lucy really didn't want to quit; she was just discouraged. Knowing what motivated Lucy, she reminded her that Grandma and Grandpa were coming over on Friday and would love to hear her play "Rainy Day." In that instant, she went from wanting to quit to needing to perform!

Lucy practiced on Tuesday. She still missed the note. Wednesday came, and she felt as if it was even harder! On Thursday, she tried again, and her pinky still couldn't reach. When Friday came, Lucy knew she had one last practice before her grandparents arrived. Would she? Could she? Lucy gritted her teeth as she approached the pesky F-sharp, stretched her fingers as far as she could, and . . . did it! Finally, all of that practice paid off, and just in time too! Grandma and Grandpa would hear "Rainy Day" complete with a superb F-sharp!

QUESTION

How did Lucy show PERSEVERANCE?

Even though Lucy felt that her little hand just couldn't reach that note, her *perseverance* eventually paid off. She was a much happier girl afterward, knowing that she had stuck to the challenge rather than quitting.

MORE QUESTIONS

◉ How do you feel when you accomplish something difficult?

◉ How do you think Lucy would feel if she did not persevere?

◉ What have you done, or what has someone you know done, that required perseverance?

*"Age wrinkles the body.
Quitting wrinkles the soul."*
DOUGLAS MacARTHUR

*"The greatest glory in living lies
not in never falling, but in rising
every time we fall."*
NELSON MANDELA

7

Politeness

It was one of those cold late-winter days. An indoor day for certain. Elliott had just agreed to play tea party with Lucy. Usually, he would not submit to playing tea party, but Lucy had just spent the morning being his goalie for indoor soccer, so he owed her. While Lucy was setting up her tea set, Elliott was busy getting into character—as a mean old man!

Lucy poured the tea, and Elliott grunted. "It's cold!"

Lucy was appalled.

Then he proceeded to guzzle the tea down in one gulp, ending with a loud *burrrrp*!

"Elliott!" Lucy shrieked. Elliott grumbled, "Where's the cookies? I'm a grumpy old man, and I wanna cookie *now*!" Still in character, he stared at Lucy for a moment, then burst into laughter. It's a good thing too, because Lucy was about to lose her temper. Elliott explained that he was just having fun.

"Good, because you were terribly impolite," huffed Lucy. She added, "Now, let's start this over, shall we?"

Elliott, having enjoyed enough sister torture, agreed.

"Here is your tea, Mr. Houndswallop," said Lucy in her best British accent as she delicately poured.

"Why, thank you so much, Miss Moneypenny," replied Elliott.

"Cookie?" offered Lucy.

"I would be most grateful for a cookie, thank you," replied Elliott as he took a small bite, careful not to let any crumbs drop.

"It's delightful to see you again," said Lucy.

"The pleasure is all mine, and I thank you again for inviting me," replied Elliott.

They paused for a moment before both of them smiled and giggled. Now they were *both* having a very good time play-acting.

QUESTION

How did Elliott (eventually) show POLITENESS?

Elliott was being very impolite when he was playacting as the grumpy old man, but he proved that he knew how to show *politeness* later on. Being polite to others will always bring out kindness in others, whether they are toddlers or senior citizens.

MORE QUESTIONS

- ◉ How do you feel about Elliott's behavior?
- ◉ Can you recall when someone was impolite to you? How did you feel?
- ◉ What ways can you show politeness every day?

"Politeness makes one appear outwardly as they should be within."

JEAN DE LA BRUYERE

"Politeness is the art of choosing among one's real thoughts."

ABEL STEVENS

8

∽

Loyalty

It was recess at school, and Elliott and his pals were coming up with their plan to play a spirited game of Capture the Flag at lunch. Another boy, Larry, was going to play on the other team and was very competitive and sneaky. Larry was the kind of kid who would do anything to win.

Elliott could never be sure of Larry. One time, he got Elliott to lend him five dollars because he said he had to buy a get-well card for his mom. Of course, Elliott lent him the money, but Larry never paid it back. Larry's reason was, "I always thought you understood that the get-well card was from you as well. I put your name on it too." Elliott never agreed with that idea but decided right then that he would not ask Larry to repay him again. He would leave it alone. It was history.

But now, Larry was watching very closely as Elliott and his friends huddled together, working out their strategy for the game. He could see that they had something very secretive going on and could hardly control his curiosity (another one of Larry's problems). He would stroll by, tilting his ear so far to try to listen in that he'd almost fall over!

As soon as Elliott's team had finished the huddle, Larry made a beeline to Elliott to try to find out their strategy. "So, are you guys going to try an end-around play? Or a fake to the left? Maybe the old dipsy-doodle-spin-o-rama play?" Elliott just looked at him blankly. Larry narrowed his eyes in thought. Then, after a dramatic pause, Larry pulled out his secret weapon. "Remember that five dollars you gave me? If you give me your game plan, I'll give you five dollars *and* this chocolate bar."

Elliott loved chocolate, and he could always use five dollars. So, he thought hard before he responded . . .

QUESTION
How will Elliott answer and show LOYALTY?

Sneaky, nosy people like Larry can be very difficult to deal with. Elliott had done the right thing by forgetting about the five dollars Larry owed him and making the decision to have little to do with Larry. But when Larry offered him the chocolate and the five dollars, it made it easy for Elliott to remember their past problems. Elliott could have gotten angry, but he politely refused to accept anything and showed *loyalty* to his real friends.

MORE QUESTIONS

- Has your loyalty ever been tested?
- Whom and what are you loyal to?
- Do you know someone who is loyal?
- Sometimes we say that dogs are loyal. What could we learn from them?

> *"Lack of loyalty is one of the major causes of failure in every walk of life."*
> NAPOLEON HILL
>
> *"Loyalty is a feature in a boy's character that inspires boundless hope."*
> SIR ROBERT BADEN-POWELL

9

∞

Gratitude

Lucy was in a sad mood. She had just spent the morning searching for her favorite book, *Lily Lightheart.* She looked all over the house: in the darkest corners of the basement, behind every piece of furniture, even in her brother's room! As she sat on her bed looking sad, her mom entered to see if she had found it. Lucy just looked at her feet and said dramatically, "This is the worst day of my life. I have *nothing* to read!"

Mom took a deep breath. "Now, Lucy, that's not true."

Lucy realized that she was probably right as she watched Mom move over to the bookshelf and pull out *The Fire-Drill Disaster,*

The Lamb Who Liked Peanut Butter, and *Tammy's Tinky Toilet Tale.* With each title, Lucy's mood brightened. Mom reminded her that many children don't have any books at all, and worse yet, many children can't even read.

Lucy realized that she had been overly dramatic. Mom also reminded Lucy about some other things she should be grateful for. She talked about the warm bed Lucy slept in each night, the food she ate every day, and a brother, mom, and dad who all loved her very much.

"Elliott sure doesn't act like he loves me!" Lucy said with a laugh. "I guess I was just being grumpy because I misplaced my book."

She hugged her mom, and as she did, mom reached behind her back and said, "Look what I found behind your bookshelf."

Lucy's eye's bugged out as she saw *Lily Lightheart,* the book she was searching for! She hugged Mom again and said, "Thanks, Mom, for *everything.*"

QUESTION

What did Lucy learn about GRATITUDE?

Lucy was certainly being dramatic when she said she didn't have anything to read. Sometimes our emotions get the better of us, and we say things that we don't mean and that aren't true. Even though we all get upset and sad, we should always remember to have *gratitude* for the things we *do* have.

MORE QUESTIONS

- ☺ How can you show gratitude every day?
- ☺ Can you remember ever being ungrateful (even for a minute)?
- ☺ What are some things in your life that you are most grateful for?
- ☺ Do you know someone who is grateful and says it out loud?

> *"If the only prayer you said in your whole life was 'thank you' that would suffice."*
>
> MEISTER ECKHART
>
> *"Gratitude is a fruit of great cultivation; you do not find it among gross people."*
>
> SAMUEL JOHNSON

10

Truthfulness

Elliott was an avid baseball-card collector, and he looked forward to the first Wednesday in March. That was the day at school that they called Wild Wednesday.

On that one day, and only one day, every card in your pile was up for grabs. So, you would bring only cards that were expendable, cards you had multiples of, or cards you didn't think were special. But never, *ever* would you bring a prized card, because if someone named a card that you had, you *must* give it away. Elliott always made sure all of his extra-special cards, especially his "Homer Homerun" rookie card, stayed safely at home on Wild Wednesday.

Elliott made trades at recess. He made trades at lunch. He won a few cards and gave away a few. It was a great day. But just before he was to face off with Brydon, the one boy who had every card Elliott had, Elliott decided to take stock. As he did, he felt sick. Poor Elliott realized that his "Homer Homerun" rookie card was still in the pile! Elliott was angry at himself for not double-checking, but he was already face-to-face with Brydon.

Brydon laughingly said, "Okay, let's start with your 'Homer' rookie card. You'd never bring that one today!"

Elliott wasn't laughing. What would he do? Would he give it to him? Or lie and tell him he didn't have it or that he didn't mean to have that card in the pile? That might work! He took a deep breath, went with his instinct, and blurted out, "Okay . . ."

Brydon couldn't believe his eyes or his good fortune as Elliott pulled out the card. Being a true friend, he saw how crushed Elliott was and knew it had to be a mistake. He said, "Awww, I was just kidding. What I *really* want is your 'Otis Outfielder' card!"

Elliott was relieved and happily handed it over. Otis.

QUESTION
How did Elliot show TRUTHFULNESS?

Oh boy, did Elliot find himself in a pickle. He surely thought that his Homer card was gone, but as the old saying goes, "Honesty is the best policy." Of course, sometimes being honest, or telling the truth, doesn't always have a happy ending. But it's better to deal with the consequences of truthfulness rather than the consequences of lying.

MORE QUESTIONS

◉ Have you ever told the truth when it would have been easier to lie?
◉ How could Elliott make sure this doesn't happen again?
◉ Why is always being truthful a good habit to have?

> *"I've learned to trust myself,*
> *to listen to truth, to not be afraid of it*
> *and to not try and hide it."*
> SARAH McLACHLAN
>
> *"A liar will not be believed,*
> *even when he speaks the truth."*
> AESOP

11

∞

Fairness

Every year around spring break, Lucy's soccer league held their end-of-season soccer challenge. And, as usual, the round-robin tournament included referees from other divisions who were known for their good sportsmanship. One of these referees was Elliott. He felt very honored and privileged to be chosen. He really enjoyed working with the younger kids. But when it came time to referee the final game of the round-robin, he felt troubled.

Why? Because Lucy's team was in the finals! He would much rather be cheering for her on the sidelines, but here he had to referee his own sister's team. Dad took him aside before the game and reminded him that a good referee had to be unbiased, impartial, and fair. That meant that even though it was his sister's team playing, he had to make calls strictly according to the rules. Elliott bravely accepted the challenge.

The game got under way. Fortunately for Elliott, both teams were playing really well and within the rules, so by the time the first half ended, he had hardly blown the whistle.

In the second half, things got really interesting. The score was tied with just minutes left. Lucy had scored a goal and was having the game of her season. She had scored, played defense, and tried her best for the whole game, but then *it* happened. Elliott saw it as if in slow motion. Lucy was defending against another player, and as the other girl passed the soccer ball to a teammate, the ball ever so slightly grazed Lucy's hand. Elliott put the whistle to his lips as a million thoughts raced through his head in a split second. If he called a hand ball, it would be a free shot for the other team, likely a goal and a sure win. What would Elliott do?

QUESTION
How should Elliott show FAIRNESS?

Poor Elliott. He probably wished he had never been asked to be a referee for Lucy's game. But to be *fair*, he really had only one choice, and that was to call the foul. Despite so many different thoughts racing through his mind in the fraction of a second before he blew the whistle, Elliott knew what he had to do.

MORE QUESTIONS

- Do you think it was easy for Elliott to be fair? What do you think crossed his mind?
- What does showing fairness mean?
- Have you ever been in a situation that tested your fairness?
- What does it feel like when someone is unfair to you?

"These men ask for just the same thing, fairness, and fairness only. This, so far as in my power, they, and all others, shall have."
ABRAHAM LINCOLN

"The secret of life is honesty and fair dealing. If you can fake that, you've got it made."
GROUCHO MARX

12

Acceptance

Elliott and Lucy eagerly arrived at the park for their weekend Ultimate Frisbee game, only to find that it was canceled.

"What a downer!" whined Lucy.

Elliott slapped his forehead when he remembered that every fifth weekend, Coach Ronnie had a different weekend game with a group of disabled kids. He organized Ultimate Hula, which is basically Ultimate Frisbee but using hula hoops, because hula hoops are far easier to catch for kids in wheelchairs.

Elliott and Lucy were ready to head for home when Coach

Ronnie stopped them. "Not so fast, guys! You don't have to go home. You can stay and play if you want."

Elliott, always ready for sport, was about to join in when Lucy pulled him aside. "This isn't our game, Elliott. Let's just come back next week."

"I know it's not our game, but it looks like fun!" he replied.

Lucy was still hesitant and whispered, "I'm a little afraid I might hurt someone."

Coach Ronnie knelt down between them. "It's not quite as fast as your game, but I think adding you two speedsters to each team will be fun. You can really kick the game up a notch." Then he turned to the other kids. "Whaddaya say, guys, would you like two speedy players?"

The other kids yelled, "Sure!"

Lucy smiled, but she was still a little reluctant.

Elliott assured her that if she accepted the limitations of the other kids and didn't expect it to be just like their game, they would have a blast. That's all Lucy needed to hear. She jumped into the game with both feet and had a lot more fun than she ever imagined.

QUESTION

How did Elliott and Lucy show ACCEPTANCE?

Sometimes we encounter situations that we can't change, so we need simply to accept things the way they are. Elliott and Lucy needed to accept that they couldn't play their usual weekend game, *and* they had to accept that the disabled kids could only play a certain way. The end result of *acceptance* was that everyone had a good time.

MORE QUESTIONS

◉ Why do you think Lucy was disappointed?

◉ How did the disabled players also show acceptance?

◉ Have you ever had to show acceptance? How?

◉ When you encounter something you have no control over, what attitude should you try to have?

> *"Give love and unconditional acceptance to those you encounter, and notice what happens."*
> WAYNE DYER
>
> *"Happiness can exist only in acceptance."*
> GEORGE ORWELL

13

∽∾

Patience

One thing Elliott really missed about school over spring break was Pizza Day. It's weird, though, because he both loved *and* hated Pizza Day. He loved it when he got a fresh, hot slice of his favorite, ham and pineapple, or "Hawaiian-style," but he hated getting stuck with a vegetarian-style. So, when the bell rang for lunch, he raced to be first in line.

On the way, Vice Principal Beeso stopped him to tell him what a good job he had done at the last band performance (Elliott was turning into quite the flügelhorn player). Elliott listened politely and patiently till he was finished. But the instant Mr. Beeso was done, Elliott bolted to the cafeteria.

"Awww, nuts!" he said silently as he skidded to a halt. The line seemed as if it were already a mile long.

The kids were all jostling and tussling for position in line. Elliott sighed. There were at least two dozen kids in front of him, and every one of them seemed to want a wedge of Hawaiian-style pizza. Piece by piece, he watched his favorite pizza pie get gobbled up. "Oh, why didn't I just shove in front?" he wondered as yet another piece trotted off on someone else's tray.

It seemed as if hours went by, but he was finally at the front of the line, and there were two pieces left. Suddenly, Mr. Beeso showed up again.

"May I?" he asked Elliott, who knew it was a rule that teachers didn't have to wait in line.

"Of course," said Elliott, who could not believe his eyes when Mr. Beeso grabbed the last two pieces of Hawaiian-style!

Elliott sulked, resigning himself to eating the rubbery vegetarian. But wait! As if by magic, a fresh, piping-hot pan of Hawaiian-style pizza was brought in and served up right before him.

QUESTION
How did Elliott show PATIENCE?

Elliott could have gotten very upset when he saw that pizza vanishing from the tray. He could have pushed ahead to make sure he got his favorite slices. He could have impatiently cut Mr. Beeso off in their conversation, but he didn't do any of those things. Elliott had *patience*. Even though it seemed as if he was going to get a crummy deal, he ended up getting a hot *fresh* slice of pizza.

MORE QUESTIONS

◉ How many ways did Elliott show patience?

◉ Do you think you would have been as patient as Elliott was?

◉ How can you show patience in your life?

"Patience and perseverance have a magical effect before which difficulties disappear and obstacles vanish."
JOHN QUINCY ADAMS

"Genius is nothing but a greater aptitude for patience."
BENJAMIN FRANKLIN

"Patience is the best remedy for every trouble."
PLAUTUS

14

Sincerity

Lucy loved Sharing Day in her class. One day, Emma brought in her adorable white kitten named Bubs, who enjoyed giving everyone in the class a nice, wet lick on the cheek. And another time, Zachary brought in some party poppers he got from his grandma in China. Sharing day was always fun.

This day, it was Barbara's turn. Everyone was seated quietly and ready. Barbara stood in front of the class with a bag in her hand. "Today, I would like to show you something I think is very interesting," she said as she reached into the bag and pulled out . . . *a newspaper*!

The class was silent as Barbara beamed. Then one of the children giggled. Another smiled. And yet another said, "A newspaper? What a laugh!" Some other kids joined in and giggled too. But not Lucy. She saw how disappointed Barbara looked as Mr. Whalen told the class to "Pipe down!"

Barbara was so upset she ran out of the class. Lucy followed her as Mr. Whalen proceeded to speak sternly to the children who had laughed and made Barbara feel bad.

Barbara was choking back tears as Lucy said, "I thought the newspaper was cool! Sometimes my dad reads the paper and tells stories about the old days when papers were the way people got the news every day!" Barbara listened, and Lucy continued, "Who else would have thought of bringing in a newspaper? You always think of great ideas, Barbara!"

All of this was absolutely true, but Barbara wasn't so sure. She said, "You're just saying that to make me feel better, Lucy."

Lucy didn't know what to say.

QUESTION

Can you think of some ways Lucy can convince Barbara that she is SINCERE?

Lucy could see that Barbara was upset. Sometimes when people have been teased, they feel that *everyone* is going to tease them. Even though she knew she was sincerely trying to make Barbara feel better, Lucy has to convince her of her *sincerity* first. She will.

MORE QUESTIONS

- Have you ever had to convince someone that you were sincere?
- Can you remember when you last demonstrated sincerity?
- Who is the most sincere person you know?
- Why is being sincere a good quality?

> *"Faithfulness and sincerity are the highest things."*
> CONFUCIUS

> *"Sincerity, even if it speaks with a stutter, will sound eloquent when inspired."*
> EIJI YOSHIKAWA

15

Citizenship

After a great weekend visit with Grandma and Grandpa, Elliott and Lucy took the train home with Gramps. At one of the stops, they looked out the window and noticed a rotten, broken-down, deserted lot full of garbage. But they saw something else too. People in red T-shirts were hauling trash, digging holes, and planting trees. "Look at those citizens," said Gramps. "What a great example!"

"What on earth are citizens?" asked Lucy. "Sounds like the army or something!"

Elliott added, "I think it's all of us who live in a country."

Gramps smiled and explained that Elliott was right, but what *he* was talking about was citizenship, which involves actually *doing* something. "Like those good-hearted folks in the red T-shirts. They're doing something for the community."

"Like volunteers?" asked Lucy.

"Precisely!" agreed Gramps. "Being a good citizen means pitchin' in, helpin' out!"

"I'm going to be a good citizen when I grow up," proclaimed Lucy.

Gramps suggested that she didn't need to wait till she grew up—she could start showing citizenship now.

"How?" both Elliott and Lucy asked.

Gramps suggested all sorts of things, such as following the rules at crosswalks, treating others with respect, being a good neighbor, and even looking after the environment.

"Like those people in the junk lot!" said Elliott.

Lucy was deep in thought and then blurted out, "Hey, how about picking up litter after the festival at the park across from our house this summer? Would that show citizenship?"

Gramps grabbed both of them and hugged them hard. "You got it, kiddos! I hereby make you official Good Citizens of the World!"

QUESTION

How will the kids show their CITIZENSHIP?

Elliott and Lucy learned that showing citizenship means getting involved, doing the right thing, and generally being a good person. They know now that by doing their share to make their school, their community, and the world a better place, they are showing *citizenship*. Following the rules of your family and your society is all part of citizenship too.

MORE QUESTIONS

- What is citizenship?
- How many different ways can you think of to be a good citizen?
- What could you do tomorrow to show your citizenship?
- Do you know anyone who is a great example of being a good citizen?

> *"Ants are good citizens: they place group interests first."*
> CLARENCE DAY
>
> *"There can be no daily democracy without daily citizenship."*
> RALPH NADER

16

∞

Integrity

E lliott's class was working on the final assignment of the school year. It was all about dinosaurs, and it required building a model and an accompanying written report. The teacher divided the class into partners for the assignment, and Elliott was happy when he was paired with Marci. Marci got really good grades. Elliott would build the model, and Marci would look after the text. What a great split! They both got busy over the next week.

Elliott was so engrossed in preparing his model that he didn't pay much attention to what Marci was doing. The day before the assignment was due, she showed up with the written report fully typed and complete with illustrations. Elliott was impressed. "This is great, and you've used some super-big words too! This is going to get us a great mark!" he gushed.

Marci responded casually with, "Thanks, Elliott. I pretty much just cut and pasted it from the Internet. You're okay with that, aren't you?"

Elliott didn't know what to say just then, so he didn't say anything right away. Suddenly, the lunch bell rang, "Let's talk after lunch," he said.

Elliott thought and thought about it. He *wasn't* okay with copying stuff from the Internet word for word. Sure, you can read and learn things in books and online, but when it comes to a report, it has to be your own words, doesn't it? After all, he had to make the dinosaur model. He couldn't copy *that* from the Internet! Then he remembered something his mom once said: "Integrity is doing the right thing even if no one is looking." Probably, no one would find out that Marci's report was copied straight from the Internet, but *he* would know. And that wouldn't be right.

QUESTION

How can Elliott show his INTEGRITY?

Elliott began to wonder just how good a student Marci really was after working with her and learning how she did things. It can be difficult to confront someone who has done something that affects your reputation, but if you show tact, you can make your feelings known nicely and still keep your *integrity,* or reputation.

MORE QUESTIONS

☺ How might Elliott feel if he didn't say anything to Marci?
☺ What do you think he said to Marci? The teacher? His parents?
☺ What is integrity? Can you think of words to describe it?
☺ Why do you think that keeping your integrity is important?

"Don't compromise yourself.
You are all you've got."
JANIS JOPLIN

"When they come [to Disneyland],
they're coming because of an integrity
that we've established over the years.
And they drive for hundreds
of miles. I feel a responsibility to the public."
WALT DISNEY

17

⚮

Kindness

One summer day, Mom and Lucy were driving to Grandma's house, when Mom noticed a bumper sticker that said Practice Random Acts of Kindness. "What on earth does that mean?" Lucy asked.

"It means to think about doing something kind, or nice, every day," Mom replied. She went on to tell Lucy about a Web site she once saw called actsofkindness.org, which encourages exactly that. "It had loads of ideas for doing kind things for others. Like buying a pizza for a stranger or planting a tree or maybe just giving someone flowers," she said.

"What a great idea!" Lucy thought.

As they arrived at Grandma's house, she was waiting on the steps as usual. There were hugs all around as Grandma whisked Mom into the house for her famous deviled-egg sandwiches. "I'll be inside in a minute!" called Lucy.

Lucy hurried to the flower patch in front of the house. Grandma loved her garden and kept it full of the most wonderful, colorful flowers. Lucy made a beeline to the perfectly straight row of tall orange gladiolus. She grabbed a pair of garden trimmers nearby and neatly clipped off ten of them, put them in a bunch, and marched into the house.

"Surprise!" yelled Lucy. "It's a random act of kindness!"

Mom looked at Grandma with a troubled face. "Are those from Grandma's garden?"

Lucy nodded a big *yes*.

Mom looked at her Grandma, thinking the worst. "Lucy, I don't think that's quite the idea . . ."

Suddenly, Grandma broke the tension and responded, "I love them! You are so thoughtful, Lucy!"

Mom was relieved as Grandma gave Lucy a huge hug.

QUESTION
How did Lucy show KINDNESS?

Showing *kindness* to people is one of the simplest things we can do. Everyone can find an opportunity to do something nice for another person every day and can make the world just a little bit nicer by doing it. For more ideas, visit www.forbetterlife.org and www.actsofkindness.org.

MORE QUESTIONS

- ◉ Lucy showed kindness, but what choice did she make that could have landed her in trouble?
- ◉ How many different ways can you think of to show kindness at school? In your family? To others?
- ◉ Can you remember the last time someone was kind to you?
- ◉ Why is it good to be kind?

> *"No act of kindness, no matter how small, is ever wasted."*
> AESOP
>
> *"Too often we underestimate the power of a touch, a smile, a kind word, a listening ear, an honest compliment, or the smallest act of caring, all of which have the potential to turn a life around."*
> LEO BUSCAGLIA

18

Responsibility

Elliott loved sports. And he was pretty good at most of them too. His favorites were floor hockey, soccer, and basketball. But this summer, he decided he wanted to try baseball. His friend Cyrus was on a team and was always raving about it. Elliott talked it over with his parents, and once they looked at the family schedule and saw that they could fit this activity in, they agreed. Elliott could join Cyrus's baseball team this year.

Things started well. He looked great in his Douglas Park Dodgers uniform. His brand-new mitt was cool. He even liked the other guys on his team. Elliott was going to like playing baseball!

That is, until he started playing. Oh, he could bat well enough, and his catching wasn't bad, either, but halfway through the season, it dawned on him. Baseball was boring. It took so long to get up to bat that Elliott considered bringing a book, but he thought better of it. It might not look good if the tenth batter's head was buried in a Captain Underpants book.

He wanted to quit. So, he did what he thought was right and immediately sat down to talk about it with his dad. Dad listened quietly and actually agreed that baseball was not the most fast-paced sport in the world. Elliott was sure Dad would let him quit before the end of the season. But then Dad began to remind Elliott about being responsible. Elliott was already very responsible in getting himself dressed, cleaning his room, and making sure he remembered his assignments at school.

Dad asked, "What about your responsibility to your team?"

Elliott hadn't thought about it that way before.

QUESTION

What could Elliott do to act with RESPONSIBLLILITY?

It's good to try new things, and Elliott is fortunate to have parents who let him try lots of different activities. They were also good parents not to let him change his mind so easily. Even though he might not want to play baseball next year, Elliott learned that he needed to show *responsibility* and finish what he started.

MORE QUESTIONS

⊚ What is good about taking responsibility?
⊚ How can being responsible make you a better friend?
⊚ Describe some ways you can be responsible.

"Responsibility is the price of greatness."
WINSTON CHURCHILL

"Make it a point to do something every day that you don't want to do. This is the golden rule for acquiring the habit of doing your duty without pain."
MARK TWAIN

19

∽☙∽

Effort

Elliott and Lucy felt proud that their grandpa had called them good citizens for getting enthused about cleaning up the park across from their house. After the festival at the park was over, they were excited to get right to the job. That's when Dad stepped in and ruined their day, just before leaving for work. He looked out the window and noticed that the festival had made loads of litter. "I'm afraid this job is just too big for you," he said. "You're going to need at least two more kids. I think you should let the park office know what you're doing as well."

Poor Lucy couldn't believe her ears. Here they were just trying to do something good, and now Dad was making it difficult.

Elliott tried to calm her and said, "I don't think he's trying to make things harder, but if that's what Dad says, then we should do it."

"I'm not sure I even want to be a citizen now," grumbled Lucy. But she didn't mean it. She got on the phone to find help as Elliott headed over to the park office.

After what seemed like hours, Lucy arrived at the park office to meet Elliott. "I had to phone eighteen friends before I found Emily and Liam, who were willing to help. But the effort paid off, because now we're ready!" Emily and Liam beamed and held up their garbage bags.

"Not so fast," grumbled Elliott. "I've looked and looked, and I can't find anyone who works here."

"Well, it took a lot of effort to find two friends to help, so I guess it will just take some *more* effort to get permission," said Lucy. With that, they spread out to find the park manager, who was already out picking up trash. He was happy to hear that the kids wanted to help and thanked them.

QUESTION
How did the kids demonstrate EFFORT?

Elliott and Lucy weren't prepared for Dad raining on their parade. But he was right. The job was much bigger than expected. They needed more help and permission. Both of them really had the stick-to-it-iveness to complete the task. With a lot of *effort,* they made their corner of the world a better place.

MORE QUESTIONS

- How come effort takes so much effort?
- How have you shown effort?
- Give examples of how your mom or dad show effort.
- Think of a job that would take the most effort you can imagine. What is it?

> *"All the adversity I've had in my life, all my troubles and obstacles, have strengthened me."*
> WALT DISNEY
>
> *"I'm a great believer in luck, and I find the harder I work, the more I have of it."*
> THOMAS JEFFERSON

20

Empathy

It was a sunny Saturday, and the whole family was out for a walk in the city park. They enjoyed walking in the park because Mom and Dad always told stories about their visits there when they were young.

On this day, just as Dad began to tell a crazy story about riding around the park on a minibike, his cell phone rang. It was Mom's aunt calling from Europe. His expression became serious as he handed the phone over to Mom. Elliott and Lucy begged him to keep telling the story, but with one look, they knew it wasn't the time.

Mom's face turned gray as she listened and said, "Uh-huh . . .

oh . . . I see . . . when?" Soon the call was over, and Mom turned to Dad and said, "It's my uncle Walter. He died this morning."

Mom and Dad hugged. But Elliott and Lucy didn't quite know what to do. It was obvious that Mom was sad, but they had never even met Uncle Walter. Mom walked a few steps away to blow her nose and wipe away some tears.

Lucy quietly tugged on Dad's sleeve. "I can see Mom is sad about her uncle, but *I* don't feel sad. And that makes me feel weird . . . a little."

Dad wiped away a tiny tear too as he pulled Elliott and Lucy close. "I know you didn't know him. Heck, I only met him once." It seemed strange to Elliott to see Dad fighting back a tear. "Empathy, kids. Empathy. It's when you can actually imagine the feelings another person is experiencing."

Lucy scratched her head for a second, and then Elliott jumped in with, "Oh, like when I felt worried when Lucy felt worried about her lost doll?"

"Exactly!" said Dad. "Now, run over there and see if you can show your mom some empathy, okay?"

"Okay!" agreed Elliott and Lucy eagerly.

QUESTION

How could the kids show EMPATHY?

It's always difficult to see our parents cry. Usually we feel sad even if we don't know what made them distressed. In Elliott and Lucy's case, they soon learned that it was their mom's uncle who passed away. Showing *empathy* doesn't mean you *have* to cry when someone else is sad, but a warm hug can show that you understand how they feel.

MORE QUESTIONS

- How would Mom have felt if the kids didn't show empathy?
- Can you think of an example when you needed to show empathy?
- What feelings could be connected to empathy?
- Has anyone shown empathy toward you?

> *"The great gift of human beings is that we have the power of empathy."*
> MERYL STREEP
>
> *"We care how things turn out because the character cares— our interest comes from empathy."*
> JOHN GARDNER

21

Charity

On the very first day of school, Lucy returned home proclaiming, "Mom! Mom! We need a charity jar!"

Mom said under her breath, "Now, this is certainly random . . ."

Lucy continued, "Kerry's family has a charity jar, and it sounds cool!"

Mom was speechless.

"It's a jar that you put money in, and everyone in the family can do it! At the end of the month, everyone in the family gets to guess how much is in the jar, and whoever guesses closest gets to pick who gets it!"

Mom smiled and asked Lucy if she knew what charity was.

"Kinda like a gift?" answered Lucy.

"Sort of," answered Mom. "But to whom?"

Lucy had assumed that the money would go to one of the family members.

"Charity can be a lot of things, Lucy," Mom said kindly. She explained that when Lucy and her dad painted her grandparents' bedroom, *that* was charity too. And when they volunteered at the animal shelter. And when Lucy ran in the mini-marathon for cancer research and collected pledges. And even when they put their extra change in the glass jar at the ice-cream shop. All of that was charity.

"I guess that Kerry's family has just come up with a fun way to keep charity important in their household," said Mom.

"So, charity isn't just giving money to someone, it's doing something that helps others?" asked Lucy.

Mom agreed. "Now you've got it!"

Lucy smiled. "I think I do. But do you think *we* could have a charity jar too?"

Mom replied, "Absolutely! I'll talk to your dad tonight, and at the end of this month, you can be the first to decide where the money will go."

Lucy leaped into her mom's arms with a smile as big as the moon. "Deal!"

QUESTION

What did Lucy learn about CHARITY?

Lucy's heart was in the right place. There is an old saying, "It's better to give than to receive," and Lucy and her family really started to feel that way once they started using the charity jar. And it's not always about just giving money. Even if you don't have much, you can always give something of yourself to others. It just feels good.

MORE QUESTIONS

◎ How can you include charity in your life?
◎ What did Lucy mistakenly think the charity jar was for?
◎ How many different ways did Mom describe charity?

"Charity sees the need, not the cause."
GERMAN PROVERB

"The life of a man consists not in seeing visions and in dreaming dreams, but in active charity and in willing service."
HENRY WADSWORTH LONGFELLOW

"If you haven't any charity in your heart, you have the worst kind of heart trouble."
BOB HOPE

22

❧

Helpfulness

It was a beautiful, crisp autumn holiday. It was the kind of day Elliott and Lucy just loved, because it meant that after Mom's famous pancakes, they could bundle up and ride their bikes on their street, which was full of brightly colored leaves. It was going to be great! Until Dad spoke.

He proclaimed that it would be a great day for Elliott and Lucy to rake the leaves by themselves for the first time.

"But what about our bike riding?" whined the kids.

Dad assured them that they'd have plenty of time for that *after* they raked the leaves.

So, right after breakfast they got to it. They raked and raked and raked some more. Before they knew it, it was time for Mom's hot soup for lunch.

After lunch, they kept raking, but Lucy moaned, "This is going to take all day!"

Elliott surveyed the situation and decided that they could finish all the raking, and it would still leave them an hour of daylight for bike riding. They'd be tired, but there was still time for fun.

Just then, Lucy noticed their neighbor Mrs. Linden coming out to rake her yard. She was a kind old lady who was always friendly and sometimes even baked goodies for Elliott and Lucy.

"Lots of leaves this year, eh, kids?" she said with a smile as she started raking her yard.

The kids were just filling their last bag when they heard a loud "Ow!" and saw poor Mrs. Linden clutching her back in pain. They quickly ran to her.

"Oh, it's just my rickety back going out on me again. I'll just give it a rest. I can finish raking tomorrow," she said as she hobbled inside.

Elliott looked at Lucy and then at his watch. She knew what he was thinking and quickly agreed. "Let's do it!" They raked and raked her yard as sweet old Mrs. Linden smiled out her window.

How did the kids show HELPFULNESS?

Elliott and Lucy could have easily just finished their raking and continued with their plan to go bike riding, but they knew that *helpfulness* to a neighbor in need would be more important than having fun.

MORE QUESTIONS

- How do you think the kids felt after raking Mrs. Linden's leaves?
- What ways can you be helpful? At home? At school? Toward others?
- How do you feel after being helpful?

> *"In about the same degree as you are helpful, you will be happy."*
> KARL REILAND
>
> *"Act as if what you do makes a difference. It does."*
> WILLIAM JAMES

23

❧

Generosity

Lucy loved her dolls, and she had a lot to love. She had so many she could hardly count them all. And they all had names. There was Jo-Jo, Janice, Max, Cody, Anna, Mary, and on and on . . .

One crisp fall day, Elliot and Lucy, plus one of her many dolls, were at the park across the street from their house. They noticed their friend Rashid playing with a new little girl on the swings. Rashid said her name was Aza. She was a pretty girl with giant brown eyes and a smile that lit up the whole park. Even though they didn't speak the same language, Lucy wasted no time in getting to know her by playing chase-the-new-kid, push-the-swing, and hide-and-seek.

Aza's mother was nearby and occasionally would warn Aza to be careful on the playground. Lucy had to guess what Aza's mom was saying since they were not speaking English. When Lucy asked Rashid to ask Aza where she was from, he said, "Afghanistan."

"Aff-gana-who-istan?" Lucy asked.

Elliott, knowing a little about world countries, jumped in and explained to Lucy that it was a long way away.

Aza confirmed this through Rashid, who explained, "They sort of escaped from there to come here to live with her uncle. They just got here last week, and they left in such a hurry, she couldn't even bring her toys!"

With that, Aza's happy face turned very sad. Both Elliott and Lucy noticed. Lucy looked at her doll and then back at Aza. So did Elliott.

QUESTION

What could Lucy do that would show GENEROSITY?

Being generous often means being self-sacrificing. To be truly generous, sometimes you need to seek out ways to help others, even if it means giving up something you really cherish—just as Lucy would do with her doll. It's not wrong to give because you have lots to give, but true *generosity* should come from inside. Give from the heart.

MORE QUESTIONS

- Can you think of other ways in which Lucy could have been generous to Aza?
- Why do you think Aza and her family decided to leave Afghanistan?
- Tell about a time when you were generous to someone or someone was generous to you.
- For more information on Afghanistan and other world countries visit www.nationalgeographic.com/kids-worldatlas, or www.worldalmanacforkids.com.

> *"We need to help younger people recognize their own capacity to do good, and help them discover the rewards of generosity."*
> BILL CLINTON
>
> *"Gentleness, self-sacrifice, and generosity are the exclusive possession of no one race or religion."*
> MAHATMA GANDHI

24

Willingness

Hector Pilpitt, a boy in Lucy's class, was never willing to try anything new. It didn't matter if it was a food, a sport, or even a book. If it was new to Hector, he simply didn't want anything to do with it. Despite this, strangely enough, Hector was not boring.

Hector had a habit of eating only peanut butter and jelly sandwiches for lunch. To keep things interesting, though, he always managed to bite them into funny shapes. He would take little bites out of each corner of his sandwich until it resembled something else. Usually, he created things such as a bunny or a shoe, but once, he managed to chew a sandwich into the shape of a volcano and then squished jelly out of the top like lava!

Lucy liked Hector but often wondered why he was so unwilling to try new things. Hector's reply was always, "I know what I like, and I like what I know."

Just when Lucy had decided that he was completely unwilling to try anything different ever, something very interesting happened. It started to snow. The whole class looked out the window in amazement as it came down, and within minutes, it seemed to be a foot deep.

Watching the maintenance man struggle to shovel the walks, the teacher was concerned and wondered out loud, "Oh, dear, I hope he'll be able to keep up with the shoveling!"

Suddenly, Hector jumped up and said, "I'll help!" Lucy was shocked and impressed. After all, this was Hector, the boy she thought wasn't willing to try anything new. But he sure showed willingness to pitch in and help out.

QUESTION
What did Lucy learn about WILLINGNESS?

On the surface, Hector seemed unwilling to do anything. He just wasn't interested in trying new things. But, in fact, he showed lots of *willingness* when it came to helping out. So Lucy could learn two things from this story: how to be willing to help and how to be careful not to prejudge people based on knowing only one side of them.

MORE QUESTIONS

◉ What was Hector unwilling to do?

◉ What was Hector willing to do?

◉ How can you show that you have a willing spirit? At home? At school? Somewhere else?

"When a man is willing and eager, the gods join in."
AESCHYLUS

"The world is filled with willing people; some willing to work, the rest willing to let them."
ROBERT FROST

25

∽∞∽

Trust

Everyone loved Lola. She was the cleanest, cuddliest, happiest little family dog in the world. So, when Elliott and Lucy's family were heading off for their annual year-end skiing weekend, there was no shortage of volunteers in Elliott's class who wanted to look after Lola (with their parents' permission, of course).

Elliott had been very responsible in looking after Lola over the last year, so Mom and Dad told him that he could decide whom to leave Lola with. They told him that making this decision would be part of growing up and taking responsibility.

They gave him one guideline: "Choose someone you trust."

Elliott had to think hard about that. The three kids who had volunteered were all his friends. And Elliott thought, "I trust them all. None of them would steal Lola." But then he thought about what trust really meant. He began to think about his friends, about their personalities, their hobbies, and even school.

Kent always made him laugh, and he loved to wrestle, but he was always forgetting his homework. Maddy was a sweet, smart girl who had an aquarium and a perfect attendance record at school. The third volunteer, Trevor, was super-bright, and he spent every weekend and most days after school playing every sport imaginable, but he slept in a lot.

Even though they were all Elliott's friends and they were all honest and trustworthy, one of them seemed more like the kind of friend to trust with the task of looking after the family pooch. That night at dinner, Elliott proclaimed to the family, "I've decided who will look after Lola this weekend!"

QUESTION

Whom do you think Elliott would choose to look after Lola?

Elliott knew that his friends were trustworthy in the simple sense of their being good people. But there are many kinds of *trust* that he had to consider. You have to earn trust by your reputation. Someone you would trust to keep something safe such as money might not be the same person you would trust with a pet, and vice versa. When it came to choosing someone trustworthy to look after his cuddly pooch, Lola, Maddy was easily the number one choice.

MORE QUESTIONS

◎ Whom would you trust with something special?
◎ How could you show that you are trustworthy?
◎ In what ways have people trusted you?
◎ Think of ways that you show trust.

"Whoever is careless with the truth in small matters cannot be trusted with important matters."
ALBERT EINSTEIN

To be trusted is a greater compliment than to be loved."
GEORGE MacDONALD

26

Respect

Elliott was visiting his friend Engo Tanaka's house. Engo had just moved from Japan and was in Elliott's class. They were fast, fabulous friends. They both loved spaceships and collector cards.

When Engo's mom answered the door, Elliott was a little embarrassed. She was wearing a robe—in winter! Elliott was relieved when Engo jumped in and, noticing Elliott's expression, explained, "It's a kimono, Elliott! We wear them in Japan!"

"Oh, of course, everyone knows that!" Elliott said.

Elliott took it in stride, as he did when he removed his shoes and had to put on funny little socks with a slot in the toe. When Engo's mom bowed respectfully, so did Elliott.

Elliott and Engo played, space-battled, and card-traded un-til lunch. Elliott sat beside Engo, with Engo's mom and dad sitting at either end of the table.

Engo's dad bowed his head, then said, "*Itadakimasu*," and then Engo and his mom repeated it. Engo looked at Elliott, who appeared bewildered.

Inside, Elliott was thinking, "Should I? Shouldn't I? What if it's something my parents wouldn't approve of?"

Fortunately, Engo leaned over and whispered, "It pretty much means '*Thanks for this, let's eat!*'"

Elliott was relieved and respectfully joined in with "*Itadaki-masu* for me too!"

Engo elbowed Elliott with a giggle. Engo's parents exchanged a glance and a smile. They were very pleased that their son had made such a nice friend as Elliott.

QUESTION

How many different ways did Elliott show RESPECT for Engo and his family?

Elliott was faced with many unusual cultural experiences at his friend's house. Fortunately, he showed *respect* by adapting to his surroundings, and while he was at it, he learned a few things about Japanese customs.

MORE QUESTIONS

◎ Why do you think it is important to respect other people's cultures?

◎ Has anyone ever shown disrespect to you?

◎ Have you ever visited a friend who comes from a different culture?

◎ Talk about other ways you can show respect every day. To an older person? To someone with a different religion? To a person who speaks another language?

> *"To be one, to be united is a great thing. But to respect the right to be different is maybe even greater."*
> ANONYMOUS
>
> *"This is the final test of a gentleman: his respect for those who can be of no possible service to him."*
> WILLIAM LYON PHELPS

A New Year

Throughout the year, both Elliott and Lucy learned a lot about ethics. They learned some new words, some big words, and maybe even some new meanings of words they already knew. Some lessons were fun, some not so much. But all of them were valuable.

Dad always says, "You never stop learning." Mom usually follows it with a gentle elbow jab and something like, "Yeah, like learning how to pick up your socks!" But the kids knew what Dad meant.

Dad meant that even if you think you know about something or how to do something, there is always a new twist or a new way to try it. And it's the same when we learn about ethics.

Every situation is different. And so is how a family deals with it.

Dad, being a little forgetful himself, also knows that it's pretty easy to forget things, so he makes sure to remind Elliott and Lucy about what they learn in each situation. And we can too.

Because now that you've finished the book, you can simply turn to the beginning—and read the stories again!

And remember, doing the right thing and feeling good are contagious—contagious in a good way! You wouldn't want to give someone a cold, but if they catch your "do the right thing" bug and it spreads, the world will be a better place.

This year and next year, along with Elliott and Lucy, let's all try to make our world a better place by starting with *us,* because what you see on the outside starts on the inside.

Please visit www.eisforethics.com to see what's new with Elliott and Lucy!

Acknowledgments

To my wife of twenty-five years, Sandra. And also to my kids, Philip and Claire. They are the beginning, middle, and end of not only this book but all of my artistic projects. xoxo

To connecting the dots of the universe. Because of this "universal-dot-connecting," I connected with Lynne Truss, who graciously introduced me to George Lucas (yes, THE George Lucas—literary agent extraordinaire, what other one would there be?), who then united me with Greer Hendricks (my enthusiastic publisher and editor) and her son Ethan (her "associate editor"), who altogether made this great little book happen. Thank you.

To my friend and the most versatile natural artist I know, Riley.

To Walt Disney for inspiring me to tell stories and imagine.

To every child I met, and will meet, who makes me smile.

About the Author, Ian James Corlett

Ian James Corlett began telling stories at a very young age. He started with hand puppets and marionettes, which segued to a ventriloquist dummy, which leapfrogged into making animated films, then evolved into student comedy shorts, then led to creating and writing animated series and then writing this book.

Ian has written for, and/or developed, many popular children's series, such as *The Adventures of Paddington Bear, Rolie Polie Olie, Lunar Jim,* and *Rescue Heroes.* He has also created several original series, including his namesake show, *Being Ian.*

Ian is also a very well known voice actor in the world of animation, entertainment, and advertising. He is the voice of literally hundreds of animated characters, including Baby Taz of the

Baby Looney Tunes, Dad in *Johnny Test,* Cheetor of *Beastwars: Transformers* fame, and a dozen different characters, including Mr. Pop in *Dragon Tales.*

The father of two and a husband of one for more than twenty-five years, he enjoys hanging out with his kids, travel, and great food. He currently lives in Vancouver, Canada, and Palm Springs, California.

For more about Ian, visit www.ianjamescorlett.com.

About the Illustrator,

R. A. "Riley" Holt is a Canadian-based illustrator, designer, and artist who resides in Vancouver.

Riley is self-taught with no formal training in art. He has a wide range and uses many different mediums in his broad spectrum of artwork, examples of which can be seen at www.rileyholt .com.

Ian knew of Riley's artwork and asked him to design Elliott and Lucy for *E Is for Ethics* based on his exacting specifications, "Big heads! They must have big heads!" It was a perfect fit. Ian and Riley hope to work together more in the future.

This is his first book as an illustrator. Riley hopes you like his pictures!